Art in the Park

Written by Catherine Baker

Collins

Look in the park, woods or garden.

Pick things up.

Turn them into art!

All of this can be art!

oak

beech

ash

moss

Rocks and soil can be art, too.

9

You can turn shells and weeds into art!

shells

You cannot keep this art for long.

But it looks good!

This is art!

🐾 Review: After reading 🐾

Use your assessment from hearing the children read to choose any GPCs, words or tricky words that need additional practice.

Read 1: Decoding
- Reread pages 10 and 11, and focus on the word **weeds**. Ask: What sort of weed is it? (*seaweed*) How is this weed different to the weeds in a garden or park? (*you find it in or by the sea, not in the soil*)
- Turn to these pages and ask the children if they can find words that rhyme.

  page 2   goods (**woods**)   page 10 burn (**turn**)
      mark (**park**)   needs (**weeds**)
- Point to a word in the book (e.g. page 13, **looks**) and ask the children: Can you blend in your head when you read this word? Repeat for more words.

Read 2: Prosody
- Model reading a page as if you are a television presenter, using your voice to create interest. Ask the children to read in the same manner.
- Challenge the children to use a voice that makes the listener want to create this kind of art.

Read 3: Comprehension
- Ask the children to describe any art they have made using things they have picked up outside. If they haven't done this, what would they like to make?
- Discuss the title of the book with the children. Ask: Is it a good title? In what ways is art in the park different to paintings in the classroom? (*page 12: this art does not last*)
- Ask the children to look through the book to find:
  - things they can use to make art
  - where to find them.
- Turn to pages 14 and 15 and ask the children to tell you about the different art shown in the photos.